🔍 DIGITAL INSIDERS

GAMERS AND STREAMERS

BY JONATHAN AND MARIEL BARD

Please visit our website, www.garethstevens.com. For a free color catalog of all our high-quality books, call toll free 1-800-542-2595 or fax 1-877-542-2596.

Cataloging-in-Publication Data

Names: Bard, Jonathan. | Bard, Mariel.
Title: Gamers and streamers / Jonathan and Mariel Bard.
Description: New York : Gareth Stevens Publishing, 2020. | Series: Digital insiders | Includes glossary and index.
Identifiers: ISBN 9781538247518 (pbk.) | ISBN 9781538247532 (library bound) | ISBN 9781538247525 (6 pack)
Subjects: LCSH: Video gamers–Juvenile literature. | Video games–Juvenile literature.
Classification: LCC GV1469.3 B34 2020 | DDC 794.8–dc23

First Edition

Published in 2020 by
Gareth Stevens Publishing
111 East 14th Street, Suite 349
New York, NY 10003

Copyright © 2020 Gareth Stevens Publishing

Designer: Sarah Liddell
Editor: Lynn Moon

Photo credits: Cover, p. 1 Alena Ozerova/Shutterstock.com; background texture used throughout VLADGRIN/Shutterstock.com; screen texture used throughout majcot/Shutterstock.com; p. 5 LightField Studios/Shutterstock.com; p. 7 flowgraph/Shutterstock.com; p. 9 Jennie Book/Shutterstock.com; p. 13 (top) Casimiro PT/Shutterstock.com; p. 13 (bottom) Jasni/Shutterstock.com; pp. 15, 21 Joe Buglewicz/Stringer/Getty Images Sport/Getty Images; p. 19 Dean Drobot/Shutterstock.com; p. 23 (top) Jeff Vinnick/Stringer/Getty Images Sport/Getty Images; p. 23 (bottom) Gorodenkoff/Shutterstock.com; p. 25 Quality Stock Arts/Shutterstock.com; p. 27 Eugene Gologursky/Stringer/Getty Images Entertainment/Getty Images; p. 29 OHishiapply/Shutterstock.com.

All rights reserved. No part of this book may be reproduced in any form without permission in writing from the publisher, except by a reviewer.

Printed in the United States of America

Some of the images in this book illustrate individuals who are models. The depictions do not imply actual situations or events.

CPSIA compliance information: Batch #CW20GS: For further information contact Gareth Stevens, New York, New York at 1-800-542-2595.

CONTENTS

Gaming for a Living 4

The Start of Video Gaming Culture 6

The Rise of Streams 8

Going Live! 10

Next-Level Streaming 12

Types of Video Game Content 14

Going Viral! 16

The World of ESports 20

It Takes a Team 22

Streaming Exercise 24

Staying Safe Online 26

The Future of Gaming and Streaming 28

Glossary 30

For More Information 31

Index 32

Words in the glossary appear in **bold** type the first time they are used in the text.

GAMING FOR A LIVING

Most of us play video games to have fun, but did you know that some people play games for a living? Anyone can be a gamer, or someone who plays video games regularly. But some talented gamers are **professionals** who make money from playing video games.

Many pro gamers create **live streams** of themselves playing video games on websites like Twitch. Others record and edit videos about games, then **upload** them to websites such as YouTube. Some even make money by competing in video game **tournaments**! The best part is that you can watch the pros online in many different ways.

🔍 WHY A "STREAM"?

The term "stream" was chosen because of how the data flows from the gamer's computer to everyone watching the video—like a stream of water! The data isn't stored on a computer. It's meant to be watched live. Some websites, like Twitch, can save a copy of the stream so people can watch it later.

ANYONE CAN PLAY VIDEO GAMES! IT'S A GREAT WAY TO MAKE FRIENDS AND SPEND TIME WITH YOUR FAMILY.

THE START OF VIDEO GAMING CULTURE

Even though they're often competing against each other, gamers have always wanted to share what they know with other players. Before streaming or posting videos was possible, gamers would write guides on how to win against other players, solve puzzles, and beat games. These guides were then published in magazines and books.

As video games became more popular, a new hobby was born: watching people play. In Japan, on a popular television show called *GameCenter CX*, the host Shinya Arino plays games and viewers watch his funny actions as he tries to win. The show is a huge success and has been on television since 2003!

LET'S PLAY!

A "Let's Play" is a video of someone playing through a game while making funny or amusing comments. This type of video got its name because gamers sometimes start these videos by saying, for example, "Let's play *Oregon Trail*" or "Let's play *StarCraft*." The gamers who create these videos are called Let's Players.

STARCRAFT WAS ONE OF THE FIRST POPULAR COMPETITIVE VIDEO GAMES, ESPECIALLY IN SOUTH KOREA. THE SOUTH KOREAN TV CHANNEL, OGN, SHOWS *STARCRAFT* TOURNAMENTS AND OTHER VIDEO GAME COMPETITIONS.

THE RISE OF STREAMS

Internet speeds became a lot faster in the early 2000s, which made uploading and watching videos easier. In 2007, a website called Justin.tv started. It was built for live video streaming. This site allowed anyone with a **webcam** and an email address to stream all kinds of videos, from events to their daily life. At its peak, a new video began streaming every second!

By 2011, the creators of Justin.tv had made something bigger: Twitch, a website for streaming video games only. In its first year, Twitch saw about 3.2 million different visitors per month. By 2012, that number jumped to 20 million!

🔍 A RECORD-BREAKING STREAM

In 2018, professional gamer Tyler "Ninja" Blevins set a new Twitch record for the largest number of viewers on a stream. Ninja invited a football player and two rappers to join him playing *Fortnite*. Over 600,000 people watched this stream at the same time, almost doubling the old record!

FORTNITE IS ONE OF THE MOST POPULAR GAMES STREAMING ON TWITCH, WITH VIEWERS WATCHING OVER 1 BILLION HOURS WORTH OF GAMING IN 2018!

GOING LIVE!

Video games are pretty easy to live stream. With Twitch, all a gamer needs to do is set up an account, install some **software**, and start playing! Some gamers go farther—they use webcams, microphones, and special software to film themselves as part of the stream. Viewers can see and hear the gamer!

To stream a video game, the computer records the sound and video of the game, and uploads this data to a website such as Twitch. Then, the website will send that data out to viewers. Data is sent over the internet in pieces called bits.

🔍 BITS, BYTES, AND MEGABYTES

Computers "think" in **binary**. This means all data a computer uses is made of 0s and 1s. One 0 or 1 is called a bit. Eight bits makes one byte. The size of a common video is measured in megabytes. Each megabyte is 1 million bytes!

NEXT-LEVEL STREAMING

Most casual gamers only add their voice to their videos. It's even more fun to see the gamer's face as they play. Many professional gamers take their videos to the next level with a powerful computer—or two! They may also use a **green screen**, special lights, and powerful cameras to record themselves for their videos.

With a camera on their face, streamers give their thoughts on the game as they play it. They can even talk directly to their viewers, who can post comments in real time on the **chat**! People watch streams not only for the game, but also to see the gamers and how they react.

🔍 STAYING COOL

Like a lot of devices, computers can get hot when you use them. While most computers stay cool with fans, gaming computers need something more. To beat the heat, many gamers use liquid cooling, which uses tubes of liquid to cool the computer quickly. Liquid cooling is also quieter!

MOST STREAMING CHANNELS SHOW THE GAME BEING PLAYED ON MOST OF THE SCREEN. THE VIDEO OF THE GAMER'S FACE IS USUALLY IN A CORNER. THE CHAT IS OFTEN ON THE SIDE.

TYPES OF VIDEO GAME CONTENT

Have you ever been stuck in a video game and watched a video to see how someone else beat it? Videos that teach you how to play a game are called walkthroughs. Playthroughs are videos where you can watch someone play a game from start to finish. Some playthroughs are even live streamed!

Other gamers make reviews of video games—they say what they liked or didn't like about the game. Reviews can also be funny! Gameplay videos show viewers what a game looks like. If you are deciding whether to buy a game, you could watch a gameplay video to see what it's like first.

🔍 TWITCH PLAYS POKÉMON!

From February 12 to March 1, 2014, Twitch viewers played a game of *Pokémon Red* together. Over 1 million people took part in this special, record-setting stream. All the viewers could control the character in the game by typing commands in the chat. Amazingly, they were able to beat the game in 16 days!

VIDEO GAME TOURNAMENTS, LIKE EVO 2018 PICTURED ABOVE, ARE OFTEN LIVE STREAMED TOO! JUAN "HUNGRYBOX" DEBIEDMA AND ADAM "ARMADA" LINDGREN ARE *SUPER SMASH BROS.* PLAYERS WHO COMPETE AND STREAM!

GOING VIRAL!

Many gamers stream just for their friends to watch, but others want to get as many viewers as possible. This is actually very hard to do. Most streamers play for years without gaining too many viewers—this is totally normal!

Gamers and streamers looking to grow their number of followers usually know exactly what kind of videos they want to create, such as playthroughs or walkthroughs. It also helps if they find something unique about themselves that helps them stand out. For example, a streamer could have a camera on their dogs playing in the background so viewers can watch both the dogs and the games!

NICKNAMES

Most online gamers go by nicknames while they play, similar to a **social media** handle. Usually gamers will use the same nickname across all the games they play, but some like to change it up. Maybe there's a silly story behind the name, or maybe it's something personal. Either way, a nickname can be anything!

MOST-WATCHED TWITCH CHANNELS OF 2018

TWITCH CHANNEL	TOTAL NUMBER OF HOURS WATCHED
NINJA	226.9 MILLION
RIOT GAMES	99.3 MILLION
SHROUD	97.1 MILLION
OVERWATCH LEAGUE	74.6 MILLION
SODAPOPPIN	51.9 MILLION
DAKOTAZ	50.0 MILLION
LIRIK	44.7 MILLION
TFUE	43.5 MILLION
ELEAGUE TV	42.8 MILLION
LOLTYLER1	41.5 MILLION

A TWITCH CHANNEL IS KIND OF LIKE A TV CHANNEL! IT'S WHERE YOU CAN FIND A GAMER'S STREAM, THEIR PAST VIDEOS, AND EVENTS.

It's very rare, but sometimes a gamer goes viral, or gains a huge number of viewers in a short amount of time. Sharing content on social media, such as Twitter, Instagram, and Facebook, plays a big part in going viral and getting a gamer's name out there.

If a gamer finds success, whether by going viral or after slowly building viewers, playing video games can become a full-time job! It's a lot of work and can be considered a small business. But to stay successful, gamers must keep making good content. They also need to stick to a schedule, or a plan for when to post content, so viewers know when to watch.

HOW DO GAMERS MAKE MONEY?

Gamers make money a few different ways. One is through video and streaming websites, such as YouTube and Twitch. Using Twitch, viewers may pay to **subscribe** or give money directly to the gamer. Another way to earn money is through product **sponsorships**, which means a company pays them to advertise a product. Gamers can play in tournaments to win prize money too!

FANS LOVE SEEING THEIR FAVORITE GAMERS, NOT JUST THE GAMES THEY PLAY! SHOWING "BEHIND-THE-SCENES" PHOTOS OR VIDEOS OF THEIR DAILY LIFE CAN HELP GAMERS CONNECT TO THEIR VIEWERS.

THE WORLD OF ESPORTS

Just like your favorite sports teams compete in games and tournaments, professional gamers can take part in esports, or electronic sports. For example, the popular video game *Overwatch* has the Overwatch League, which is a group of 20 teams from cities all around the world. This league, or group of teams, competes every year between spring and fall.

There are also huge esports tournaments where professional gamers compete on teams or alone. The biggest tournament for fighting games in the United States is called Evo. It includes *Super Smash Bros.*, *Tekken*, *Street Fighter*, and other popular series. Evo started in 1996, making it one of the longest-running esports tournaments.

🔍 THE PROS SPONSOR ESPORTS

Many video games are based on sports, such as basketball or soccer. These games are so popular that some major league sports teams sponsor their own esports teams! The owner of the Los Angeles Rams and Colorado Avalanche owns an esports team called the LA Gladiators which plays *Overwatch*!

BENJAMIN "PROBLEM-X" SIMON BECAME THE FIRST BRITISH GAMER TO EVER WIN THE *STREET FIGHTER V* CHAMPIONSHIP AT EVO 2018! EVO IS SO POPULAR THAT EVEN ESPN REPORTED ON PROBLEM-X AND OTHER BIG WINNERS FROM EVO 2018.

IT TAKES A TEAM

Playing video games, running a streaming channel, and sticking to the schedule of a professional gamer takes hard work. Like with most sports, it helps to have a great team of people you can practice with. Teams of gamers have formed all around the world, and these teams usually play one or more games together.

Groups such as Cloud9, Team SoloMid, and Team Liquid have many members and compete in tournaments for all different games. Team Liquid, for example, has over 60 champion-level members across 14 games! Professional teams like this have managers, coaches, and team captains, just like other sports!

JOINING A PROFESSIONAL TEAM

It can be pretty hard to get a spot on a professional esports team. Gamers who want to join have to be very good at the team's game, and they must be great team players. Playing in online tournaments is a great place to start for someone looking to get noticed by a top team!

TEAMS CAN BE DIFFERENT SIZES, DEPENDING ON THE GAME. FOR EXAMPLE, *LEAGUE OF LEGENDS* TEAMS HAVE FIVE PLAYERS.

STREAMING EXERCISE

People love playing video games so much that more activities are being turned into games—even exercise! A company called Zwift makes indoor cycling (or bike riding) into a video game of sorts. With a **virtual** bike on a virtual road, cyclists can ride at any time in any weather.

Zwift is so popular that it now has an esports league, called the KISS Super League. Top cyclists log in to Zwift and compete in races, just like they would in the outside world. These races are live streamed!

🔍 SHOULD YOU ALWAYS BE STREAMING?

Sometimes when streamers are just getting started, they feel they must "always be streaming." But this can get exhausting very quickly! It's important to balance work and free time. Even though they're playing games, streaming can still be a lot of work, so gamers should set limits on how much time they stream.

THIS BIKE EXPO FAIR IN THAILAND IS JUST ONE EXAMPLE OF HOW COMPETITIVE VIRTUAL CYCLING IS BECOMING MORE POPULAR AROUND THE WORLD.

STAYING SAFE ONLINE

All this activity on the internet is awesome! But gamers should know the risks of putting themselves out there for people to watch. When gamers or streamers become popular, just like other stars, they can be flooded with good and bad messages from viewers. It's important not to share too much personal information online, such as where you live or your full name. This is another great reason why streamers use nicknames!

Streaming sites such as Twitch have rules about what gets posted and what viewers can comment. Twitch and YouTube set the lowest age to use the sites at 13 years old (with permission from parents).

🔍 WATCH OUT FOR TROLLS!

Although the internet is a wonderful place to enjoy hobbies and play games with friends, some people use the internet in unfriendly ways. These people might leave mean comments, try to ruin games, and be rude to play with. It's a good idea to ignore or block negative users.

THE STREAMY AWARDS, THE SHORTY AWARDS, AND THE GAME AWARDS ARE JUST THREE EXAMPLES OF AWARDS FOR GAMERS AND STREAMERS.

THE FUTURE OF GAMING AND STREAMING

The most exciting thing about online gaming and streaming is that the possibilities are truly endless! You can be a gamer just for fun who streams right at home just for your friends to watch. Or you can work hard to become a professional gamer who competes in huge tournaments in the world of esports. And the best part of all this: There's room for everyone to play and share the games they love with each other. Whether a stream goes viral with thousands of viewers or it has only a couple of faithful followers, the most important thing is that people enjoy playing and watching games!

🔍 MAKING GAMES WITH STREAMERS IN MIND

As gaming and streaming technology gets better and better, video game makers are thinking not only about how to make the game fun to play, but also about how to make it fun and easy to watch. Game makers are adding cool new camera angles, video replays, and all sorts of fun extras for viewers to enjoy.

BEING CREATIVE AND MAKING GOOD CONTENT FOR OTHER PEOPLE TO ENJOY CAN MAKE BEING A PRO GAMER AND STREAMER A FUN JOB!

GLOSSARY

binary: a two-number system computers use for storing data and making calculations

chat: a messaging system that allows users to post comments in real time

green screen: a green background used to create certain special effects in movies and videos

live stream: to transfer data in a continuous way, meant to be watched immediately

professional: earning money from an activity that many people do for fun

social media: forms of electronic communication that allow people to create online communities to share information

software: a computer code, or program, that instructs a computer what to do

sponsorship: a person, business, or organization that provides money to, or sponsors, a player or team in order to help them compete

subscribe: to follow a user or organization online for free or for payment in advance

tournament: a sports competition with many players or teams, usually taking place over multiple days

upload: to send data from one computer to the internet

virtual: being on or simulated by a computer

webcam: a device used to capture video of someone while on a computer

FOR MORE INFORMATION

BOOKS

Lyons, Heather. *Programming Games and Animation*. Minneapolis, MN: Lerner Publications, 2017.

Guinness World Records. *Guinness World Records: Gamer's Edition 2019*. New York, NY. Penguin Random House, 2018.

Paris, David and Stephanie Herweck Paris. *History of Video Games*. Teacher Created Materials, 2016.

WEBSITES

Esports Kids
www.esportskids.com/about
An online community for kids looking to play video games in a competitive yet safe environment.

Youth Esports of America
www.youthesportsamerica.com/
Online organization for your future high school esports clubs and teams.

Common Sense Media
www.commonsensemedia.org/lists/new-kids-video-games-2019
Find the coolest new age-appropriate games to play!

Publisher's note to educators and parents: Our editors have carefully reviewed these websites to ensure that they are suitable for students. Many websites change frequently, however, and we cannot guarantee that a site's future contents will continue to meet our high standards of quality and educational value. Be advised that students should be closely supervised whenever they access the internet.

INDEX

Arino, Shinya 6
awards 27
Blevins, Tyler "Ninja" 8
cameras 12, 16, 28
computers 4, 10, 12
DeBiedma, Juan "Hungrybox" 15
esports 20, 22, 24, 28
Evo 20
Fortnite 9
gameplay 14
Justin.tv 8
Let's Play 6
Lindgren, Adam "Armada" 15
limits 24

liquid cooling 14
money 4, 18
nicknames 16, 26
Overwatch League 20
playthroughs 14, 16
reviews 14
rules 26
Simon, Benjamin "Problem-X" 21
teams 20, 22
Twitch 4, 8, 10, 11, 14, 17, 18, 26
YouTube 4, 18, 26
Zwift 24